That Certain Blue

Poems
By
Sharon Lask Munson

Blue Light Press ◆ 1st World Publishing

1st WORLD
PUBLISHING

San Francisco ◆ Fairfield ◆ Delhi

That Certain Blue

1ST WORLD LIBRARY
809 S. 2nd Street
Fairfield, IA 52556
www.1stworldpublishing.com

BLUE LIGHT PRESS
1563 45th Avenue
San Francisco, California, 94122

BOOK & COVER DESIGN &
INTERIOR ILLUSTRATIONS
Melanie Gendron
www.melaniegendron.com

COVER PHOTO
Keith Munson "Afternoon Light"

AUTHOR PHOTO
Keith Munson
munsonkeith@gmail.com

FIRST EDITION

LCCN 2011918660

ISBN 9781421886299

For my husband Keith
my biggest fan

and for my sisters
Nina and Bonnie
who remember Burlingame Street

and
in loving memory of my parents
Bernice Lillian Silverglade Lask
Leon Arthur Lask

Acknowledgments

Thanks to the editors of the following journals in which these poems appeared, sometimes in alternate versions.

Denali: "Charleston", "Springtime in the Willamette Valley"
Drash Northwest Mosaic: "New Year Gift", "Then She Goes and Writes a Poem"
Earth's Daughters: "Summer Dress"
Groundwaters: "After Saturday Market", "Glimpse Into a Marriage"
Herstory Anthology: "Depression Generation"
Manzanita Quarterly: "Oh, Mom"
Mid or l'dor: "Savoring"
Modcloth: "Button, Button"
New Verse News: "Citizen"
Poetica Magazine: "A Gift from Rothschild", "Belief", "If By Chance There is Memory in Your Slumber"
Popshot: "First Street Elementary"
Punkin House Digest: "Forewarned", "Into the Half-Light", "Generations", "Traces of the Critic"
Quizzical Chair Anthology: "Ensemble"
Sandcutters: "Biking to Mazama"
Silver Boomer: "Pearl Harbor", "The Way of It"
Thema: "Last Supper"
Threshold: "Epiphany"
Verseweavers: "Torta di Mele"
Windfall: "Anchorage Recess"

Table of Contents

1. Feathering Down

2. Sketches

3. Other Footprints

4. Six Years

5. Passing Landscape

1

Feathering Down

Torta di Mele

It all begins in the kitchen
with the sifting of fine grained flour.
A powdery softness blankets my hands,
film of white circles the bowl,
coats my starched clean white apron.
I'll cut parchment, line the pan,
crack open fresh brown eggs,
peel apples, slice them thin,
layer sprinkles of lemon,
a teaspoon of vanilla, shakes of cinnamon.

Tonight we'll be in Tuscany
silvery moon full—
leading us up remote hill towns,
through threadlike pathways
and ancient cobbled lanes.
I'll stroll the Ponte Vecchio,
drift past fine-grained marble statues,
rest beside a dry Artesian well
with you, my darling
pressed together, arms laced
sipping brawny wines
greedily spooning heavy sweet torte.

The Sky, that Certain Blue

Day's end
dinner on hold
a chilled bottle of white,
the sky that certain blue
swirls of indigo, streaks of slate
the kind of hue
that brings a wistfulness.

Sounds carry—
through open windows
automatic sprinklers
shower the lawn next door,
a ten-year old turns a corner skateboarding,
the scrape and chafe
of metal on cement,
vies with strains of Chopin.

Two Great Blue Herons
fly over old oaks
bound for the Delta Ponds,
their own nesting mood
not unlike ours
splashing, earthbound
end of the day
feathering down together.

Fragment

I try not to think of the splinter
wedged in my index finger,
remains of a day spent gardening,
piling brush, pulling weeds.

I can't look at the needle probing
beneath the high intensity light,
the magnifying glass set at an angle.

His head is bent beneath my chin,
his fine blond hair
graying now, soft as down.

I think of his tenderness,
his hands that have known other places—
gently now,
as a butterfly alights.

Lovers' Pantoum

We make love in the morning
slowly, our greeting to the day
with the sun just coming up
shadows and cobwebs of night erased.

Slowly, our greeting to the day
forgotten in this measured dream
shadows and cobwebs of night erased
a quiet dance at dawn.

Forgotten in this measured dream
we perk coffee, butter toast
a quiet dance at dawn
muse about the wind-blown day.

We perk coffee, butter toast
all day walk snug
muse about the wind-blown day
safe, in the pocket of your warm.

All day I walk snug
with the sun on high
safe in the pocket of your warm
we made love in the morning.

White Space

I

I sit in the kitchen and listen.
Rain pours through branches of tall oaks,
soaks the ground,
puddles pathways.

I note the pulse
of whirl and rumble
coming from the basement,
feel warmth
circulate through floorboard heaters,
hear the start and stop
of the mail truck beyond the hedge.
Down the street
notes of a violin resound.

II

Elsewhere
the first salmon
reaches its birthplace upriver,
a painter rests his brush,
peaches ripen, fall unnoticed,
herds of zebras
canter across a narrow ravine.

Somewhere a mother
braids her daughter's hair,
a tulip yawns, bends,
gifts are opened,
a string of pearls break and scatter,
lovers sleep.

Somewhere an argument is settled,
a thread is knotted,
ground shifts,
Earth rotates on its axis
and a vine maple drops its last red leaf.

Nocturne

Downstairs, silk drapes are drawn,
pillows are carefully positioned
plumped-up on the button-back sofa.
Red hothouse tulips
stand upright in clear glass.
A fountain pen rests, tightly capped
on an unfinished letter,
blue-black ink on vellum.

Silverware and serving pieces
dried and put away
wait for breakfast within kitchen drawers.
Green pears picked the day before
ripen in a shallow bowl,
persimmons on the sill.
A tattered joker
bookmarks a new volume of poems.

Outside, a soft drumbeat
falls against the front door
as early morning news lands on Welcome.
Footsteps recede down the front walk.
A gypsy moth opens its wings
lands on the paper, wanting in—
two hours until daybreak.

Tiptoeing back upstairs,
I slip into my side of the bed,
glance at the waning moon
through gabled windows,
hear the owl in the madrone,
drift.

Springtime in the Willamette Valley

The neighbor's chestnut tabby
drinks in sunlight outside my kitchen window.
We inspect each other warily
through mud spattered double pane glass.

On the lawn a redbreast robin scouts mown grass
stalking a savory morning snack.
The puss turns its head, wary and watchful.

The sapphire sky spreads out
like a child's picture book,
its pages pillowing clouds
clothespinned in suspension.

Winds from the south
whisper to yellow daffodils,
their long necks bent toward the open gate.

Soft breezes dry freshly laundered shirts
clipped to the line in back.
Purple lilacs along Priceboro Road
fill the air with perfume.

In the school yard
an eight-year-old soars high in a swing.
Ever mindful, in the distance, the Coburg Hills
stand like soldiers
guarding this gentle valley.

Full Throttle

Southbound I-5
we tear into the fast lane
pass fields, winter drab
sheep in pastures, mud splattered,
Century farms, dormant, set back.

Chuck Berry's voice spills
from Classic Rock Station
KJMX, 99.5 FM.
I move to the music, seat belt straining
fingers strumming, singing along—
you, loving the driving
the open road
freedom of a fast car
turn up the volume.

We pass nurseries closed for the season,
flocks of Trumpeter Swans overhead,
newborn lambs on grassy slopes
shakily bent toward their mothers.

Sliding close on the bench seat
I slip off my shoes
rub the smooth burnished leather
of your freshly polished cowboy boots.

Meadowlands give way
to rugged hilly terrain.
We weave our way up the mountain

traveling the highway, visibility clear
throttle up.

Then She Goes and Writes a Poem

She creates his favorite
macaroni and cheese,
rich, creamy, a trio
of Gruyere, Asiago, sharp cheddar

and he enthusiastically suggests, again
after thirty-eight years of marriage
this casserole would be great
with a hamburger on the side.

She doesn't respond as she places
the hot breadcrumb topped dish
on the round maple table,
simply reminds him to uncork the wine
as dinner is ready.

If he were Jewish, she knows
he'd never suggest mixing milk with meat
or request chicken gravy
or parmesan topped veal cutlets,

and although there are times
she indulges herself with soft-shelled crab
from Newman's Market,
or spicy shrimp scampi
from her favorite downtown café,
she has certain sensibilities.

She pulls out a chair
spoons the golden pasta
onto plain white china and raises a fork.

After Saturday Market

I color-coordinate my vegetables
into bowls of unexpected shades and hues,

sight and taste mingle in a dance of colors
like blue flax and scarlet poppies

cresting along the highway,
tints of blush on the edge of a bend

bursting forth with honeyed pleasure.
Ruddy, sugar-coated beets

thick, smooth as velvet
spill into plum colored basins.

Crunchy pole beans drowse in amber crocks.
Blood-red tomatoes

thickly sliced, show off on white bone china,
while tender young carrots idle in cobalt.

Plump corn on the cob, lightly steamed
waits impatiently for a light slathering

of sweet yellow butter.

Eve of Rosh Hashanah

I put away summer,
reach for the cooler days
of Rosh Hashanah's new season.
Golden leaves free fall,
pine cones tumble.
I inhale musty smells
of brush and bramble.

I'm remembering another autumn,
my father at forty
zipped into a well-worn brown leather jacket
wooden rake in his hand,
slight against Midwestern elms.

Overhead Canada geese heading south,
stop briefly.
I pull my sweater close,
slip hands into deep pockets,

reflect on the year's passing
joys and sorrows
good deeds and bad
an unkind word, an apology.

Attentive to the day,
the wind carries
short blasts of a ram's horn

sounds of the Shofar
ushering in a new year.

Winter of the Neon Horses
a pantoum

Bone chilling, bitter weather
bleak, raw, rainiest recorded
along sixty-five miles of I-5
fifteen life-sized sculptures tarry.

Bleak, raw, rainiest recorded
horses, dazzling night's gloom
fifteen life-sized sculptures tarry
through Oregon downpours, dense fog.

Horses, dazzling night's gloom
headlights, like Saturn's rings
through Oregon downpours, dense fog
miles and hours from nowhere.

Headlights, like Saturn's rings
stallion spirits out of shadows
miles and hours from nowhere
along Oregon's dark, starless highway.

Stallion spirits out of shadows
behind fences, in fields
along Oregon's dark, starless highway
visions of Arabian, Mustang, Palomino.

Behind fences, in fields
outlines in vivid fluorescent
visions of Arabian, Mustang, Palomino
white, cadmium yellow, threads of aquamarine.

Sure, staunch, steadfast mounts
along sixty-five miles I-5
conveying courage, resolve
bone chilling, bitter weather.

Evenings at Five

Something sensual in the way
he uncorks wine,
pauses as it scents the air,
views its ruby tinge
as he tilts the bottle
toward natural light
spilling in through kitchen windows.

Something seductive
as he chooses vintage stemware,
pours the Cabernet
into ample goblets,
watches it stream into clear crystal,

hints of berry, plum, currant
suspended over ivory tile.

2

Sketches

Charleston

My mother danced the Charleston
on a summer's day
when I was young.
Stepping back
she raised her arms
and began, oh so slowly
fingers cupped, body taut.

Hesitantly
she began to move with more abandon—
knees high, hips turned,
heels tapping,
shoulder straps falling,
apron flying,
smiling and laughing.

My mother danced the Charleston
around the dining room table
while the soup simmered
and the day lengthened,
with work to be done
and a house to run.

My mother danced the Charleston
as I edged into the shadow of the buffet,
wide eyed.

A Gift from Rothschild

My father, age twelve
had tea with Lord Rothschild
the family story goes—
part of the vast Jewish emigration
out of Belgium, into England
as World War I enveloped Europe.

Baron Rothschild
invited immigrant children
for afternoon tea
held in the grand foyer
of his private museum.
Dad, small, reserved
dressed in his only white Sabbath shirt
stood shyly in the center of the hushed hall,
sipped his sweet tea,
nibbled thin dry biscuits.

As the hour drew to a close
and day turned to dusk,
Rothschild wandered among the boys and girls,
murmured a kind word,
tousled a head—
gently pushed away the cup
my father thought to hand back.
Give it to your mother,
the nobleman said,
Tell her it's a gift from Rothschild.

Savoring

Friday afternoon
one braided challah
sits on the kitchen counter
still warm from the oven.
Chicken soup simmers
onion, bay leaf.
Mother's hands pluck chicken
peel carrots, cut parsnips, stuff helzel.

I watch from a white wooden chair.
My mother's speckled apron is loosely tied.
Damp curls escape a tight set,
her gold earrings fly in rhythm
to the beat of the well used wooden spoon.

We rest, reach for the bread
fold carefully, spooning.
Mother's filled with crispy fried grebenes,
mine the tasty browned onions.
We munch, savoring the end of work for the week
in anticipation of the Sabbath.

Deck of Cards

Joey Silver and I sit upright
on his mother's green metal chairs,
protected from the summer sun
by wide awnings covering the front porch.

I shuffle and deal.
His two aces crown my queen.
One brown oxford drops
and then the other

along with a matched pair
of tan Brownie socks,
red plastic bar-shaped barrettes,
two yellow hair ribbons
leaving braids unfurled,
my first watch, received
the morning of my eighth birthday,
a treasured Sky King secret decoder ring,

my last five pennies lost to Joey
gambled away, one at a time—
all that was left
from my week's allowance.

With my worldly possessions
laid out on his door mat
I gather them back,
and like an itinerant peddler
ready to head down the road,
rubber band my cards,
and walk the half-block home.

Mad Money

Dad would slip a few coins
into my Mother of Pearl evening bag
socked away for an emergency,
a quarter, a few dimes, some nickels,
next to the lipstick holder
behind the powder puff.

Enough for a phone call, he'd say—
my knight, if needed
ready to slip behind the wheel
of a pink and gray Dodge,
slay the dragon.

I never called
but, oh, the security, the trust.

Early Morning

She sits alone,
gazes at icicles
hanging low from the eaves,
listens to their clear ringing,
winter's peal

sips the last of the Earl Grey,
eyes the clock above the stove,
watches the minute hand
circumnavigate on its hourly trip.

She calculates minutes left
before the house becomes
rowdy with voices of children
summoning, demanding—
flush of the toilet,
slam of drawers,
buzz of her husband's electric shaver,
drum of feet down the stairs.

She tightens the belt on her quilted housecoat,
selects radio station WJR,
turns on morning news,

reaches for the box of Cheerios,
a second cup and saucer,
plugs in the coffee,
drops thinly sliced
bakery-bought rye into the toaster

glides into another winter day.

Depression Generation

Mother saved her weekly allotment
in heavy brown envelopes
taken from my father's store—
each pouch titled in her large flowing hand
Egg Lady, Dry Cleaners, Milkman.

She was ready when women from outlying farms
knocked on the side door
to deliver warm brown eggs,
or when the milkman brought
cheese, butter, cream.

She was prepared to pay the newsboy
for the daily Free Press,
Mr. Grossberg's delivery van
for freshly baked seeded hard rolls.
I watched Mother budget her pennies.

Decades later I will clean out her apartment,
bring down from upper shelves
one rose-colored lace nightgown wrapped in tissue
still in its gift box,
slips too lovely and fragile for everyday wear.
In her bottom dresser drawer, I discover
nylons, still packaged, in the sheerest of shades,
black elbow-length gloves, just in case.

I kneel on worn yellowed carpet,
crush delicate fabric between my fingers,
bury my face, breathe in smells of talcum
mixed with the fragrance of Coty's L'Origan.
I rock back, the familiar room encircles.

Glimpse Into a Marriage

They drift to the porch after dinner,
the still of evening heavy with scent
from hollyhock and moonflowers.
They seek a flutter of cool
after a day dense with heat.

He, tie off, white shirt-sleeves rolled,
she, in a flowered housedress,
slide into warm metal chairs
the day's *Detroit News* between them.

She picks up the Home section
the pale light of lavender shadows at dusk—
tears out recipes, breaks their silence
to share aloud, *Dear Jane Lee.*
Next door intrudes.
Amos and Andy spill
from the Hackelman's open window.
Shrill sounds of a streetcar slice the hush.

She places her hand on his arm.
He folds back the front page,
comments on President Truman,
offers opinions on Korea, the Rosenburg trial,
takes both sides of the problems
at Henry Ford's River Rouge plant.

Twilight fades. He fills his pipe
loosely packing his favorite Dunhill London.
She rises, steps inside to check on children sleeping.
When she returns streets lights are on,
stars emerge, the waning moon, a slender arc.

They welcome night's darkness,
hear the trill of crickets,
watch fireflies flit beyond the hedgerow.
No one sees their hands laced,
fingers braided,
or the kiss he plants on her palm.

Pearl Harbor

His first new car
purchased from a dealership
near Woodward and Second—
a bitter cold Saturday
December 6, 1941.
An economical sedan
stripped down, two-door
green Plymouth.

During the war years
he'd stop at bus lines,
streetcar tracks,
any corner a serviceman waited
with a thumb extended.

He'd drive downtown
picking up sailors,
war weary soldiers, marines
home on leave

use his prized gas rations
for those fighting—
drive them to a mother's arms,
lonely barracks, or a local USO

contributing in the only way he knew
for owning the last car sold in Detroit
until the men came home.

At the Bowl-A-Drome

My father permits me to
skip Temple Israel's
Sunday morning religious school—
instruction in Hebrew,
Jewish ritual, holidays,
Israeli song and dance,
smatterings of ancient history,
in exchange
for tagging along at the Bowl-A-Drome.

Dad's bowling league
joins the ongoing cacophony of rolling balls,
clattering of the automatic pin setting machines,
Jailhouse Rock, blasting from the sound system.

Tenth frame mojo—
notwithstanding gutters and low scores
I watch my hard-working, non-athletic dad
pick up his ball,
move toward the lane with a look of concentration
and single-mindedness,
bend his knees, pausing
before moving forward
and letting it fly.

Released, the ball picks up speed
and with a slight hook
shoots down the wooden alley,
hurls itself smack into the right pocket,
explodes into a strike.

Among cheers and back-slaps of the team
I clap loudly from my spectator's bench.
Engulfed in the magic of the moment
I think it quite possible
God is hanging around
sipping bottles of Vernors,
nibbling Clark bars,
manufacturing miracles,
playing hooky, too.

Dreaming Burlingame Street

Stepping over cracks in the sidewalk
I land on squares stamped
Detroit Public Works,
see again old neighbors
relaxing on wide front porches
shielded from the summer sun
by striped canvas awnings.

I dream of familiar two-story brick homes,
narrow driveways, one-car garages,
tidy rectangles of green grass.
On the corner of Linwood
I stop in front of the apartment building
bordering Mr. Haney's ice cream shop.

Carole Sue's black and white terrier
runs between parked cars.
The 1956 blue Buick that will strike Pepper
sits in the new car showroom
at the dealership on Gratiot.

Michigan's dreaded elm disease is years away.
The thick canopy of green over the street
casts shadows as day lengthens.

Mr. Mittelman is walking
toward me. I wave,
no longer the timid child
fearing his doleful moods,
his formal way of speaking

or the numbers tattooed
on the inner side of his left forearm.

Snapshot in Sepia

She stands on a rooftop
somewhere in New York
Brooklyn or Queens—
head turned
ignoring the camera.

Her filmy flapper dress drifts.
Light winds whip delicate flutter of silk.
Her short hair, brushed flat
peeks out from under a light colored tam.
She peers into a looking glass.

I never knew her then, eighteen
pocket-sized mirror in her left hand,
powder puff or lipstick in her right.

The mother I knew didn't fuss
painted her lips freehand
never missed the lines.

Generations

Now that we are old ourselves
Mother and Dad gone,

Max, Rose, and all the other aunts and uncles buried,
we remain the ones left to remember

the soft glow of the night-light
making shadows in the upstairs hallway,

the underground tunnel
beneath the Powerhouse on Linwood,

the roll of the swinging bridge—
the sudden shock of the first chilly plunge

off the wooden raft into Lake Huron,
the splash, ruffling its waters.

3

Other Footprints

Kismet

In middle-age
they combine households,
each having endured tragedy

a long-drawn-out death
hospitals, hospice, desperation,
divorce after twenty years
fury, accusations, trepidation—

casual friends in common
a last minute invitation
dinner, a symphony

and in that hopeful season they begin—
find a small house
combine warm knotty pine
with cool Danish modern,
his dining set, her white sofa.

Rummaging through his musty boxes
and her files of ancient history,
she casually hands him
a black and white snapshot of herself

the Catskills, five decades earlier
swim suited, sunburnt, pigtailed—
one of a dozen ten-year-olds
playing kickball, jumping rope.

He clasps the tattered photo
before raising his eyes,
points to a slim boy standing apart
slightly behind the fuss and uproar
and stunned, softly says, *That's me.*

Summer Dress

Now that we're older, I'll invite her.
If she'll come, I'll ask her to pack
the blue and white striped seersucker dress,
the two-piece, with tiny pearl buttons enclosing the front.
I'll ask her to bring the dress she wore so long ago,
that summer she loved me.

That season we spoke of cherry festivals
and the making of jam.
We pored over Pearl Buck stories
and other books we both loved.
We lit the grill, laughed at the memory of hot dogs
over an open fire on the shore of Lake Huron.
We were companions at the kitchen table
while the Earl Grey cooled
and the hands of the clock moved forward.

That summer I played in the sandbox with her children,
shoveled my own dreams into red plastic buckets,
rolled miniature cars along ruts in the driveway,
pushed wooden swings straight up to the sky.

If she comes, I'll brew sweet lemon tea.
We'll stroll narrow garden paths
so our shoulders sway and brush.
We'll wander tiny shops,
pick up cut-glass bowls we don't need or desire.
We'll let the years slip away,
walk with a spring to our step
and be girls again.
And if she comes, I'll ask her to pack
the old blue and white summer dress
she wore one season so long ago,
that summer she loved me.

31

Fences

For years it was coming to this,
loose boards leaning in light winds,
splintering, too weak
for occasional pots or hanging baskets.
Yesterday, the old fence came down
rotted through, folding into itself.

Today, for the first time
I look out at neighboring yards,
expanses of silken grass,
yard after yard, meadow-lush, green.
A fat periwinkle hydrangea
and a mid-summer clematis
shyly introduced, lean together
like new lovers under the morning sun.

My view is heightened
by hedges of wild roses tumbling, spilling out
under my neighbor's kitchen window,
for me to enjoy, but just for today

as the builder will arrive precisely at nine
with hammer and nails,
truck piled skyward with newly cut boards
that will divide again, pound apart,
neighbor from neighbor
to continue our lives
alone, together.

Stray

for Jane and Norval

They spied the black dog,
late morning, in the walnut orchard.
Go home she shouted. *Away.*

They observed him again, that evening
behind the new barn
scrawny, rawboned, clearly a stray.
She put out a bowl, scraps from dinner.
He came to eat when they left
wary, keeping his distance.

Perhaps, the couple considered,
this animal knew other humans
anger, a boot, a strap.

Within weeks the dog crept closer
circumspect, heedful of a hand
accepted a piece of steak from an open palm.
Later, a bone to gnaw.
Slowly the dog filled out
responded to a touch, a stroke.
No further than the porch, she insisted.

They had vowed no more pets
after the children left.
He wanted no bother.
She, a farmer's daughter
spurned animals in the house.

They named him Stray.
Brought him in one bitter night
where he curled up beside them.
Good dog, good boy.

Button, Button

She snips off blue plastic buttons
before donating her husband's worn
denim to the local thrift,

removes silver studs
from her now unfashionable gray silk,

lops off metal fasteners from jeans, jackets,

trims tiny seashells
that hold together the lightweight yellow dress
worn three summers ago.

She slips the array of buttons
into her nearly full bell jar,
admires the blend of colors,
the mix, the diversity,
runs her fingers through the cool collection

while the impoverished, the needy
already lost inside the turmoil of disarray,
pore through overflowing racks at Goodwill
searching for closure.

Inertia

She squeezes the sack of flour
against her chest, lets out the air,
stands transfixed.

Outside, October's leaves drift, a jumble
of copper and rust against the screened-in porch.
Black-throated sparrows feast at the backyard feeder.
Next door, a neighbor peers
from behind half-closed curtains.

She presses, dreamlike
oblivious as the boys cut through the kitchen,
argue over crayons and rulers,
gather schoolbooks, jackets.

The woman crushes the bag to her breast
as the striped tabby brushes her ankle
and the minute hand on the kitchen clock
moves forward.

Suspended in time
she floats through early morning
slowly, slowly, a rowboat without oars

awaiting a current of wind
while the long ties of her cotton robe unwind,
braid themselves by the draft of floorboard heaters.

The Craftsman

for Chris

At ninety-three, bent with age
he stands beside his young grandson,
tidies his basement work bench
everything in place—
wrenches, pliers, bevels,
drills hung, according to size,
and the ancient turn-screw
his own father gifted him on his tenth birthday.
He blinks in the dim
admires the almost finished birdhouse.

The boy rubs the rough slabs of bark,
eyes questioning.
The man gestures.
The lad nails the pitched roof into place,
adjusts the three-inch overhang,
grins at his grandfather.

Alone, the old gentleman recalls
rocking chairs, breadboxes,
intricate carvings on cribbage boards.
In the distance he hears
the beat of a hammer,
the new birdhouse being placed.
He is pleased.
It is done.

Chicken Cacciatore with Hunter Sauce

The woman slings bags of groceries
along a scrubbed tile counter,
glances at the kitchen clock,
slips thighs and drumsticks
under running water, shakes sharply,

recalls her mother
bemoaning the monotony
of fish, beef, or fowl,
the tedium of every night,

considers running away,
daydreams—
a simple apartment in town
or a modest cottage by the sea,
chilled Chablis at a corner café,
a light cheese soufflé,
rich bowls of thick bean soup,
starched white linen, attentive waiters.

She hears a key in the lock,
splashes oil into a pan,
chops sweet onion, peppers, mushrooms,
minces fresh garlic,
sautés as she gathers tears

adds diced tomatoes, a splash of red,
sprinkles of basil, rosemary, parsley.

Fluttering curtains
that frame the open window
grow still
as she scatters dustings of thyme
and acceptance.

The Way of It

A man gets used to things
scent of a woman, her skin, hair
hands perfumed with onion, bay leaf
neck stretched, a nesting crane
as she peeks through small-paned windows
searching winter skies.

A man gets used to life
head bent to sacred writings
a wooden chair, a bench
glasses of lemon tea

obeyed by his children
but distant from the chatter and joy
of their fleeting childhoods.

A man gets used to seasons
ciphering days and dreams
walking narrow pathways
as autumn leaves
mark the year's passing.

He teeters on a tightrope
unsteady jobs, a hopeful handshake
the comfortable sameness of town—
the teacher, the butcher, the shul
a skullcap, as faint as clear mist
as weightless as the one thin strand of hair
that drifts toward first light
and morning prayers.

Citizen

It's not the hand that signs the laws
that holds the destiny of America.
It's the hand that casts the ballot.
—Harry S. Truman

I don't vote
the woman proclaims smugly
as the plane approaches the gate.

Every morning she crunches numbers
buying and selling stocks and bonds,
ciphers margins,
scribbles numerals in plump portfolios
while slowly sipping her favorite
vanilla-flavored double-latte.

She never steps into a voting booth
or assumes responsibility,
lives comfortably on the twenty-fifth floor
overlooking the park,
her dark-green, late-model Citroën, is garaged
for getaways and country weekends.

She spurns political discussions,
never watches debates
or studies candidates running for office.
She doesn't think political parties stand for her.
She never agrees
and both sides are wrong.

She speaks out against school bonds
as her children are grown,
rejects branch libraries
and rapid transit,
talks down America,
is out of town for elections—

boards planes easily,
packs lightly, flying to foreign shores,
extols the virtues of café crème and Camembert,
peppers her conversation with a little French
and a spatter of Italian,
makes herself at home in the world
as she tangos from border to border.

Ensemble

The diners
are passionately
devouring—
but it is the cook

peeking
through swinging doors
who feels
the fullness

of roasted duck
in plum sauce,
a generous man

softly swinging
his wooden spoon,
like a conductor

at the helm
of woodwind and brass.

Old Guys

They crowd into the café
flicking away snowflakes
February's biting cold

marking their appearance
startling customers
hefting chairs, scraping floors
pushing tables—
prefabricating the boardroom of memory
directors of little, violating the quiet

buddies from Center Sports, showing off
relaxing after yoga, weights, showers
finishing up with decaf and chat.

Monday's hyperbole
embroidery of rumor, speculation
heart monitors, Saturday's game
a mother's death at twenty-six, five decades earlier
their ages, oldest to youngest
MSNBC
twenty-thousand a year in the 1950's
conference calls, train schedules
Mariners in Seattle
trucks, sales tax
monthly Rotary dinners.

They gather together
male voices rising
baiting, pulling chains
a camaraderie of old guys
topping off the morning.

Still

They still have their sunny
second floor condo in Boca Raton,
summers at the family home up in Maine.

She hasn't yet
hidden the string of pearls
behind out-of-date chops in the freezer.
So far, he's not depressed, lamenting
he's in the wrong place,
has to go home.

And although the Saltines
in the cupboard are stale,
the frozen chicken pot pies
each night, monotonous
the children haven't gotten involved.

They still fool the world,
drive their old red Camaro,
find their way across town
to doctors, the dentist,
afternoons of gin rummy,

tiptoe into warm water
at South Beach, their steps
leaving footprints in damp sand,
glance furtively around
to see if anyone's looking.

Winter Study on an Early Morning Walk

Fog
dense at dawn
cloaking daylight.

I am attentive
to the distant ringing of icicles,
how they toll in the frozen air.
Bare oaks hang suspended.
Briars, honeysuckle, wild grape
all subdued.

Out of view, in the bottom of the stream
frogs slumber far below the ice.
Bumblebees hibernate within loose bark
waiting for lengthening days.
Ground squirrels safely rest in their lair—
close to a towering snowman.

The quiet of morning is splintered
by random flute-like echoes
of the spotted wood-thrush,

in the river below
a lone kayaker
presses on, ghostlike,
soundlessly weaving, blindfolded
down the swiftly moving creek.

Who Loves

She wore a simple gray dress
pink carnation pinned
carried a lace hanky.
He wore a dark suit and tie
stood stock still,
a wild thing drawn to light.

The wedding table held
yellow-layered cake,
bottles of whiskey,
Barton's chocolates,
gifts—
white percale sheets,
matched pots and pans,
a small milk-glass dresser lamp.

They moved into a sunny
four room apartment
that smelled of yesterday's pot roasts.
She would slice
plump cucumbers, radishes,
warm, red, vine-ripe tomatoes,
serve dinner
on plain white dishes
from the five and dime.

He read the Daily Gazette,
listened to major league baseball
on the Philco console.
Black and white sketches
hung on their wall,
still life of fruit, Paris in the rain.
Shelves were filled with her books.

He was good to her,
got down on his hands and knees
scrubbed her kitchen floor.

They barely touched
no accidental brushing of shoulder,
but sat side by side
smoking Camels, flicking ashes.

Traces of the Critic

I question
if he had written poems of his own—
left in drawers,
stored in boxes, attic, cellar,
snippets, scraps, pages tagged,
corners folded in lined notebooks
filled with closet verse.

After a lifetime
critiquing the celebrated
and the obscure,
did his unspoken words exist?
What fine-tipped pen, set to paper
recorded his own story?

Belief

We move back and forth
on old porch rockers,
legs tucked,
lazily watching the sun disappear
behind the crumbling cow barn—

and in the span between day and night
she tells the tale of her father
who didn't believe in Jesus.

When he told her such a truth
she was amazed
and with twelve-year-old sensibilities
questioned, *Then are we Jewish?*

I laugh this day
under the black walnut trees
the two of us friends
going on forty years,

that brief exchange
beginning and ending
our only
conversation on religion.

Junior High Tough

Slicked-down black hair, dark eyes
made Jesse Handler a bit mysterious.
A clever boy, confident
he sauntered down hallways
with an aura of naughty.

I left school each day
through the west side entrance
far from the office,
the exit, adjacent to the softball field

bearing down on the same metal handle
Jesse jostled to meet his friends.
I'd stare at him
hanging out, looking cool, smoking Camels.

He held his cigarette
Humphrey Bogart style
between thumb and forefinger

didn't inhale, but kept it burning
leaving gray ash on home plate.

Forewarned

You are about to forget the red rose bush
that blooms each May on your birthday,
ingredients for the tart lemon pie
you serve on fine blue china,
and the touch of our mother's cool firm hand.

You reach for slippery names,
forgotten titles, mislaid books.
You tape reminders of daily appointments
on bare white walls,
stare bewildered in front of grocery shelves
torn between stewed tomatoes
or canned peaches swimming in sweet, thick syrup.

Slivers of a puzzle you try to recall
lie scattered, strewn between
cracks in the sidewalk
we jumped over as children.

Roads you used to travel easily
are now slightly beyond reach.
I see you at the crossroads, adrift,
off course in an uncharted realm.
I am forewarned.

4
Six Years

Epiphany

White sheets in the wash,
dark towels in the basket.
Shall I put on the coffee
the woman questions,
again,
as her daughter emerges
from the cellar.

Was it the indirect gaze
or something in the glance?
The room is suddenly in shadow.
Branches outside the window
brush the pane.

She sees on her mother's face
lines that have deepened,
hair that has thinned.
She feels the future
in the quiver of a lip,
the blink of an eyelid.

She opens her arms,
cradles the older woman,
reaches inside for the strength required.

Who is the mother?
Who is the child?

Into the Half-Light

I see her in the distance
barefoot, slowly shuffling
down the long corridor.
Hospital walls cold and flat
match the white of her fine hair.
Her pale-green gown
knotted loosely on top
swings open in back.

Mama, I cry out.
Mama, wait.

She turns at my voice,
confused.
She stares, lost and fearful.

Awareness slowly pierces
the fog of memory.
Her arms rise as I race down the hallway,
reach and clasp her to me.

She looks up, shyly smiles,
places her palm on my cheek and asks
Are you my mother?

If By Chance There Is Memory in Your Slumber

In sleep, do you slip-slide back
recall me, your blue-eyed daughter
fine brown hair braided, ribboned.

While you drift
are you back in the red brick house
peeling parsnips, plucking chicken
lighting Friday night candles—
or are you a child yourself, clutching tightly
to your own mother's firm warm hand.

I enter your narrow bedroom
glimpse the hills of your body
under the blue flowered afghan,
your snow-white hair matted, tousled.
You stir, utter sounds I can't unravel.
It's been a year since we last spoke.

I settle myself comfortably
on the padded rocker,
gaze out the window at the gray sky,
listen to thunderstorms pummel the roof,
throaty black crows in the yard
flapping, cawing.

Where do you go when your eyes close?
Is your mind the empty slate
that greets you upon wakening.
Or if by chance
there is memory in your slumber,
I wish you, my darling Mother,
the sweetest of dreams.

New Year Gift

A year has passed
since she last spoke.
Loss of language is part of the disease I am told,
often happens with Alzheimer's.

On daily visits I chatter.
Spin tales of her grandchildren,
report front page headlines,
read out loud articles
from *Good Housekeeping*,
letters from *A Bintel Brief.*

Today I arrive early,
greet Mother with a hug.
Shanah Tovah, Mama.
A sweet New Year!
I toss off my jacket,
slip it on the back of a chair.
It's Rosh Hashanah, Mom.
I made honey cake, I add,
peeling Glad Wrap
off the small package.
We are in the kitchen,
the sunniest room,
Mother's place of choice.

Today she doesn't respond.
Doesn't open her arms.
Her fingers play with tassels
around her turquoise shawl.
She sits forward, rocks.
I go to the sideboard, pour myself
a cup of coffee. Pour a second for her.

Cut the cake into bite size pieces,
sip my drink, observe
a squirrel on the fence in the yard.

Out beyond the patio
I spot finches feeding,
notice hydrangeas turning
from bright summer blue
into steel-gray of autumn.

I give Mother a kiss on her cheek.
A sweet New Year, Mom.
Today is Rosh Hashanah.
I was a good girl
went to services last night
standing room only—
you know how it is on High Holy Days.
And while I was there,
I had a long talk with God about you.

Slowly Mother turns. She puts down
her small piece of cake.
What did he say? she questions.
Her voice after so long, was surprisingly strong.
I feel tears, blink them away.

He says you are comfortable and without pain.
You are getting wonderful care
and you are in the best place possible.
He says things are as good as they can be.

Mother replies conversationally,
Well, isn't that nice.
Isn't that lovely.

Again she begins to speak,
her words, jumbled.
I listen carefully.
Did you say Anna?
Mother nods.
Aunt Anna?
Mother nods.

There's Anna, Jean and Fay
I say, stunned we are having
a true conversation.
She speaks.
There's one more.
I begin again.
There's Fay.
There's Jean.
There's Anna.
And there's Bernice.
Mother nods as I add
her own name to the list.

At noon lunch is served.
We are quiet as I sit with her.
Soon it is time for an afternoon nap.

I reach for my jacket,
kiss her good-by.
I'll take another kiss, Mom.
Take two, she responds.
I kneel
put my arms around her slender shoulders,
kiss her again. Twice.
I love you, I say.
She bends her head, puts her lips to my hand.

Last Supper

When she no longer ate
only sipped water
I chopped one spring onion
until my tears ran free,
stirred in bits of sweet pepper, tomato
and sautéed slowly
a panful of love.

I whisked and fried
one small brown egg
into a golden omelet.
We sat at the table
soothed by the familiar aroma
of the savory sauce.

I grasped the spoon
and stretched my arm.
Her mouth quivered.
Eat little bird
little wren, my sweet
and bite by bite, chewing slowly
she eyed me through narrow slits
relishing at the end of her life
a Spanish omelet, her favorite meal.

Oh, Mom

I clean out shelves in my linen closet
where I store bath towels, sheets,

and the few things left that belonged to you.
I reach far into the back, behind clutter

and extract your beige shoes
the ones you wore toward the end,

lace up oxfords, extra deep
with the scuff on the side where they rubbed.

It was the scuff that brought me down,
that jaunty clip to your walk.

Yahrzeit Candle

In memory of Mother

The constant flame
lit last evening
still trembles in the quiet
of early morning.
My bare feet slide,
silk against white-oak floors.

Alone in the flush of dawn
elbows on the kitchen counter
I lean into shadows
welcome the silence—
not wanting to share this moment
with filling the kettle, brewing tea
or early morning news.

The candle flickers.
My palms encircle warm glass,
a fragile beacon at sunrise.
Memory drifts to another time,
another kitchen—
shimmering candles
honoring grandparents I never knew,
aware of the generations
as this ancient tradition continues.

Streetlights snap off. Morning
filters through cotton curtains—
the candle will burn until sundown.
She is with me
as I open the front door, reach
for the paper.

A neighbor walks his dog, waves
and I begin to move
into the light of a new day.

Roses on Her Birthday

I'll carry home
from neighborhood florists
long stemmed yellow roses—

call to mind the golden climber
that bloomed each May on her birthday,
fragrant blossoms clambering outer walls,
carpeting small-paned kitchen windows.

I'll trim stems
fill cut-glass with cool tap water
place brilliant flowers on blue tile.

I see her still,
parting curtains
gazing out.

Snowstorm

1

White sodden tissue
not easily peeled
from dark cotton fibers
were always in her clothing
during those years with me.

I found them on her navy skirt,
inside seams of summer dresses,
deep in the bottom of apron pockets.
Looking for hidden matter,
I probed and prodded
seldom outwitting the snowstorm.

2

Today I open the Kenmore
pull out my own damp mounds of
dark shirts, colored socks, black slacks,
all flecked with white fragments—
like the aftermath
of a frigid polar squall.

Tiny pieces of rolled lint
hide deep in the cavern of a vest
or in the coarse twill of favorite jeans.
I look around and cry out, *Mom?*

5

Passing Landscape

A Moment in Jerusalem

On a narrow street off Nahalat Shiv'a
a snow-haired woman
sits on a folding chair
between an open door
and pots of fragrant lavender.

With a sweep of her arm
she beckons me over,
grasps my hand.
Her raspy voice
speaks words I can't fathom.

I kneel as she chatters,
never slowing for a reply.
I point to my chest, speak my name.
She beams a toothless grin,
plays innocently
with the silver band on my watch.

Another woman approaches,
pantomimes batty—her index finger
drawing circles by her ear as she shrugs.

I brush my lips against the gnarled cheek,
give her a tender hug.
Is she bestowing wisdom of the ages?
Telling me of Cossacks galloping
through her Russian shtetl eighty years earlier?
Reciting tales of a young girl's prayers
never reaching heaven?

Or perhaps she simply imagines
I am a neighbor dropping by
and grateful for the morning visit,
speaks of mild weather
on such a cloudless spring day.

An American Question

So, you like it here?

Nadia knows immigrants never ask
each other these questions,
is aware her answers
in the plodding English
she barely understands
would take too long

trying to explain
her lonely one room apartment
facing Greyhound's main terminal,
the tasteless frozen pizza
she purchases at all-night supermarkets
after coming home from the late shift
at the care center.

Still, she loves
the new blood-pressure monitor
she bought cheaply at Sears
to send to her cousin in Sarajevo.
She loves aisles of shiny kitchen gadgets
and gleaming refrigerators,
expects if she works hard
she, too, could speed down I-5
in a used Ford Fiesta.

Nadia shrugs
as she watches fireworks displayed
high over the ballpark
on her first Fourth of July,
and responds,

It's good.

Back to the Living

Tell me once more of your brother
of young Joe, who vanished from Auschwitz
with only a crude rucksack
filled with a half-ration of dry bread,
two shriveled turnips, a moldy potato,
a stolen spool of wire,
a spoon, a rough-hewn knife,
and a grimy green tattered sweater
upon his gaunt shoulders.

Joe, who stole away
from the crammed wooden barracks
after evening roll call,
after floodlights had passed over
and the Germans turned
to light their cigarettes
or take a piss—

Joe, who on a starless, cloud filled night
clawed his way
into the cold Polish dark
well beyond the guard tower,
stumbled from one birch tree to another
as the moving branches
rushed forward to embrace him.

Sunday Afternoon at Golders Green Park

London, England

I

We eat a simple breakfast
white coffee, hard rolls, marmalade.
The narrow screened-in porch
shows dark blue,
mid-summer hydrangeas gone wild.

The London Underground is blocks away.
Rose charges out the door,
revived after a night of disco,
turns left on Dartmouth Road
toward the Bakerloo Line.
Her pink dress
shows off long shapely legs,
her head down, as if studying lines in cement.

Jill follows, checks a white clematis
from a low hanging vine,
ties the long sleeves
of her mint-green sweater
around slender shoulders.

I am the American observer
in love with English gardens,
green-grocers, the sweep of the Thames,
Soho, Chelsea, Piccadilly—
crazy for this novel slant to my summer.

Mohan follows at the end, older at twenty-six
tie-less, his navy blazer
casual, but for his bearing.
He had arrived on time for breakfast.

Now his serious brown eyes turn humorous.
Our skirts blow wildly as the train approaches.

At the crowded White Swan
we order warm tap beer, sausage rolls,
a ploughman's lunch—bread, cheese, pickle.

Beds of old roses peek out from behind stone terraces,
fishponds ripple, lovers on blankets kiss.
We meander between water-lily ponds.

Day lengthens.
Rose and Mohan slip away.
His right arm circles her waist,
her head rests against his white shirt,
his lips light her hair.

We return at dusk,
open front windows.
Edith Piaf's voice fills the flat,
spills through the evening.
I splash an inch of Drambuie
into a goblet.

II

In six months London fog drapes Golders Green.
Mohan departs, a flight to India,
family obligations, a promised bride.

Rose rushes to Calgary, red-eyed.
Jill advertises for roommates,
unaware Alan is hovering
just beyond this junction.

With summer gone,
I accept a job eighty miles east.
Packed and ready, my steps slow.
I lift my dark blue duffel,
slowly shut the door.

On the Line

in loving memory of Julia Thorne Jolley

She positioned auto parts in their proper places,
installed engines, seats, dashboards
building Dodges, Plymouths, DeSotos,
repetitive, tedious,
an ache in her wrists, down to the tendons

worked forty hours a week
on the assembly line,
time and a half, weekends.
Up with the sun,
boarding the Woodward streetcar
while the wakening city clamored around her—
home in time for the sixth inning at Brigg's Stadium,
a chilled can of Vernors beneath a cloud of weary.

Chrysler's Highland Park plant—
punching in, punching out
dressed in hard-toed shoes and bib overalls,
swinging her black metal lunch pail
on time for the day shift

paying off the mortgage on a two bedroom home,
her paycheck spread thin across the bread of days,
sending a few dollars each month back to Ireland
and a few pennies more, faithfully
dropped in church coffers each Sunday.

Toward the end of her days
given a hard earned promotion
like catching the brass ring,
a coveted prize
driving brand new Chryslers
off the assembly line
and steering them proudly out into the yard.

Passing Landscape

for Keith

He tells me he still recalls the scent
of his 1940, pea-soup green
two-door Ford Sedan,
gas and exhaust perfuming the air,
the sweet aroma of burnt oil
during hot Iowa summers
staining driveways
and narrow country roads.

Gas, twenty-four cents a gallon
at the Cut-Rate Station on Lincoln Highway,
two dollars worth to Fort Dodge and back
or trips downtown
for Maid-Rites grilled with onions
on plain white buns.

The radio antenna on the front fender
provided the music—
always the music.

Windows wide
as updrafts of air
merge with bursts of freedom
and the cadence of being seventeen—

all is the moment
the passing landscape.

August Night at Crater Lake

Perhaps it is
the full moon,
or the wind

as it whispers
through spruce
and fir,

or the clouds
as they curl
over Wizard Island,

or the stillness
of this one starry night
that makes it ours for the taking.

Cross Country in March

We leave a Best Western
somewhere in Kansas,
slipslide the icy lot,
head west on I-70,
the highway, fit only for skaters.
Ice droplets frost the windshield.

We pass a tan four-door Chevy
over-easy in a ditch—
slow to fifty, forty, thirty-five,
pull ahead of a U-Haul
on its side in the median,
furniture, clothing scattered.

Ten miles further
a tractor-trailer rests in a heap
blocking the passing lane.
That's it my husband mutters.
Truckers know how to drive—
turns on his right blinker
exits the interstate at the first off ramp
heading into Oakley, Kansas

ten in the morning
places the credit card
on the last room to be had in town,
an old ma and pa motel,
double bed, thin towels,
twelve inch black and white TV
on a swivel stand, one maple rocker
covered in brown tweed,
a sign over the door, giving Welcome.

We pick our way gingerly
across the slippery path
to the overcrowded truck stop café.
Over the clamor and hullabaloo
of other waylaid travelers
order tall mugs of black coffee,
short stacks, fried eggs,
maple syrup,
and peppered bacon on the side, crisp.

Sixty Seconds Along a Pennsylvania Highway

Every man dies—
not every man really lives.
—William Ross Wallace

I

On a Harley
twenty miles east of Scranton
the man's head slumps left
followed by his shoulder.
The bike veers, in sync
over the rumble strip
beyond the white lines,
strikes a guardrail,
sails.

II

Below the roadside
in the Lackawanna River
a rainbow trout rises,
its broad reddish band
and silvery sheen
all grace and movement.

The fish soars into the air,
snags a mayfly in mid-flight
before swimming steadily
back to where the current runs fast,
silently vanishes
into the bottomless deep
of his pool.

Anchorage Recess

Tall and lean
like a solitary silhouette
against expanses of white—
he stands knee deep in snow,
pant legs tucked, hands gloved,
parka zipped, its hood pushed back, exposing
his freshly shaven face to bracing cold.

Nine below zero
at the foot of the Alaska Range—
swings and slides glisten in the hoarfrost.
Frozen ground, the length of the playground
reveals ruts made by sleds.
The dark green of spruce and fir
cradle mantles of snowfall.

Knowing a hundred pair of eyes
are watching from classroom windows,
he holds the tin dishpan
outstretched in his left hand,
the stainless steel spoon in his right

and begins to beat, striking
powerfully and swiftly
pounding, pummeling
walking slowly and deliberately
unaccompanied by alarm—
until the bull moose turns,
walks off the playground,
lumbers across Patterson Road,
and heads to the neighborhood beyond.

Our leader
raises his hand for the all-clear
and the primary children
sweep out to morning recess.

Bear Lake, Alaska

1

North of Talkeetna
past Trapper Creek trading post
we stop for a tank of Tesoro
and a snack of jerky.
The proprietor offers to fly us into the bush,
Bear Lake for the weekend
thirty minutes by plane.

No people, he says
but a tight one-room cabin
a boat, some canned food.
He'll pick us up Sunday.

Trusting, we park our small trailer
behind the single gas pump,
lock the red Scout,
and wing our way in his four-seat Cessna.

2

Dew covers the boat.
The sullen sky baits a hesitant sun
as we zip up, pull on caps
push off into chilled water.

Stillness as we paddle
makes us speak softly.
A pair of loons pass,
their wailing, the haunting cry of the north.
Lake trout and grayling rise,
beavers at the narrow end of the side channel
slap and slide.

Later we pan-fry fish
on a propane stove,
open tins of beans, creamed corn, Alberta peaches.

We fall asleep, entwined
under dank Hudson Bay blankets
oblivious to the dazzling July light
of the midnight sun.

Another Deep Creek Morning

Rapidly changing tides
keep them vigilant,
these summer tourists
who arrive with their forty foot motor homes
bearing out-of-state plates,
noisy generators, pressure cookers,
glass jars, tin cans, all stockpiled.

They harbor schemes to smoke and can
their daily salmon catch
by the light of the midnight sun,
unconcerned they will
hold captive and keep awake
the rest of the campground.

Early morning, and the tide book
gives license to launch,
no mention of the difficult channel into Cook Inlet,
or the long narrow sandbar at the head of the river—
and as the tourists' pristine, flat bottomed boats
lie swamped in Deep Creek
filled with water,

the seasoned Alaskans
survey the ebb and flow
well past its perfect slack-tide,
sip cups of Folgers,
nibble jelly doughnuts,
scan the flat horizon.

Kenai River Running Wild

Gloved, capped, swaddled in rain jackets
they sit low in the boat
shoes and jeans soaked with spray
while above, the brooding sun bullies them
above gun-metal clouds.

Fighting swift currents
the boat careens from shoal to shelf.
The man rows cautiously
away from birch branches
skimming their heads,
massive rocks,
tangles of fallen trees and sweepers
that would snare, flip them over
into bitter cold.

The woman rises on her knees,
her rod, tight, bent like an archer's bow,
the red of the spinner
firmly snagged in the salmon's mouth—

a sheen of silver
beneath the glacier-fed
milky green torrent.

The huge Chinook, firmly hooked,
struggles and spars
while she holds on
trying to guide the great fish in.

Glimpses Into My Alaska

I tell them of the romance
of thirty foot tides
along Turnagain Arm
at the mouth of Bird Creek,

seductive cool summer evenings
beside Potter's Marsh—
attentive to the cacophony
of warblers, juncos, arctic loons,

massive ice-covered
snow capped peaks
crowning Alaska's Wrangell Mountains,
silhouettes at sunset.

I tell them how the Glenn Highway
descends into the valley
of the Matanuska River,
the milky color of its great glacier,

glimpses in January
of large flocks of Ptarmigan
garbed in white winter coats,
veiled and inconspicuous—

hoarfrost on clear, still, freezing days
coating surfaces of tree branches
wires and poles—
translucent in the winter sun.

I tell them of the sockeye run in July,
trout-like Dolly Varden,
sixteen-inch grayling
caught in late afternoon,
grilled over a campfire for dinner.

But what I can't explain
is the wildness that surfaces
as I launch my dory
from the wide-mouthed
boat harbor near Ninilchik
into the silver-blue windswept river—
cresting over pearl-gray waves
that carry me into the sound.

How I hunker down
where sea and land
come face to face,
intersect my own
untamed hungers.

First Street Elementary

Early September.
The children enter, toting
stiff new book bags
filled with lined notebooks,
number two yellow pencils,
boxes of sharp crayons.

How earnest they are
scrubbed and combed,
their clean new sneakers
squeaky
as they trek down
brightly lit hallways.

And all through the morning
mothers, at home,
move through silent rooms,
listen.

Biking to Mazama

I pedal steadily, bent low
arms outstretched, head down, back level.
The road to Mazama slopes sharply uphill,
surprising me. I breathe in, exhale.

Washington's Highway 20 heads
over rolling hills, high desert—
paintbrush and larkspur surround,
sagebrush covers my path,
cars whiz by, honking
as I flit along the narrow shoulder.

Drafts of winds whip my dank hair.
I spit bugs, swat black flies,
wipe droplets as I steadily climb.

My cadence breaks over loose gravel.
I wobble, falter,
calf muscles tighten, thighs brace.
I pedal standing, gaining momentum
as I top the last hill, elated, determined
to win the hard earned downhill sprint.

I'm twelve again, fourteen
feeling a freedom long forgotten
watching the odometer climb
as the wind cools—
fifteen miles an hour
twenty, thirty.

Exalted, I fly
fingers light on the handlebars
letting the bike take me, laughing.

View of Central Park West on New Year's Eve

Peal of crystal,
fragrance of Worth,
the song of chopsticks on the baby grand—
young men turned-out in suit and tie,
girls black sheathed
from Bonwit Teller, Saks,
hair showered in sparkle.

Dark blue velvet drapes drawn open
lay bare the city.
I linger at the window, transfixed
by the canvas below,
swirls of white spiraling,
feathery flakes,
winter's trimmings.

Thirty-two floors down
pedestrians navigate slushy boulevards,
horns and sirens muted
intermix with Neil Diamond's *Beautiful Noise*.

Streetlights illuminate
swarms of New Yorkers,
heads tucked, hands pocketed.
Beyond the crowd
mounds of fresh white snow blanket
bushes, benches, bronze sculptures.

All is glitter, reflective light.

Downward Progression

I stop in the upstairs hallway
as the sun makes its way
into the dim corridor

notice the slant of light coming to rest
on a single nail,
a slight spike, flat-headed
hammered into the guestroom door,
a peg unnoticed for years.

I am jolted back
to the time she lived with us—
an oversized pink-flowered straw bonnet
chosen with care, prominently displayed

hung there, to alter her downward progression
of that mean, life-changing disease,
helping Mother recognize her own room.

On the Verge of Slumber

I'm blanketed in down,
sleep, just heartbeats away.
A poem pops up, unannounced,
a refrain repeated,
a word, a first line,
midnight.

I thrust a bare arm into the air,
grope along the nightstand,
track notepad, pen,
shiver
as blasts of wind from an April storm
hurry in through open windows.

Hunkering back under,
I retreat from meter and rhyme.
Eyes close
as I fall into the arms of Morpheus
vowing
to remember the strains of my new poem
in the morning.

About the Author

Sharon Lask Munson grew up in Detroit, Michigan. She attended Michigan State University and Wayne State University. She taught for the Department of Defense Schools in England, Germany, Okinawa, and Puerto Rico. After overseas teaching, Sharon drove her blue Oldsmobile up the Alcan Highway to Anchorage, Alaska where she put down new roots, taught school, married, and lived for the next twenty years. She is now retired and lives with her husband, Keith, in Eugene, Oregon. She has poems in *Verseweavers, Windfall, Earth's Daughters, Drash: Northwest Mosiac, The Quizzical Chair, Goose River Anthology, Popshot, Punkin House Digest,* and many other literary journals and anthologies. Her chapbook, *Stillness Settles Down the Lane* was published in summer 2010 by Utterred Chaos Press. *That Certain Blue* is her first full-length book of poems.

Printed in the United States of America